Farm
Animals, Work, and Life

By
Camille Babeau

Illustrated by
Charlotte Ameling
Hélène Convert
Ilaria Falorsi
Camille Roy

twirl

Contents

? The "Let's Review!" pages at the end of each section help reinforce learning.

Index Quickly find the word you're looking for with the index at the end of the book.

Look for the colored boxes in the bottom right-hand corners. You will find references to related subjects in other parts of the book.

On the Farm

The Farm

On a farm, the farmer can raise animals and plant fruits, vegetables, and grains.

greenhouse

solar panels

fruit orchard

vegetable garden

farmhouse

shed

poultry yard

pickup truck

garage

courtyard

farm equipment

sheep pen

car

road

path

scarecrow

hay

barn

pasture

storage silos

cowshed

hay wrapped in plastic for storage

paddock

pigpen

field

How
do you become a farmer
?

Do you like growing plants or being outdoors, in the fields or with animals? If you do, you may like to be a farmer.

People often become farmers because they have family who work on a farm. That way they learn the job from their relatives.

You can also become a farmer by training in agricultural work. Visiting an educational farm is a good way to find out more about farming.

Farmers Market **60**
Educational Farm **72**

Tractor

Tractors often pull equipment used for plowing, planting, fertilizing, and harvesting crops.

revolving light

side mirror

exhaust pipe

steering wheel

fender

engine

headlight

running board

driving wheel

wheel rim

counterweight

front wheel

compact tractor

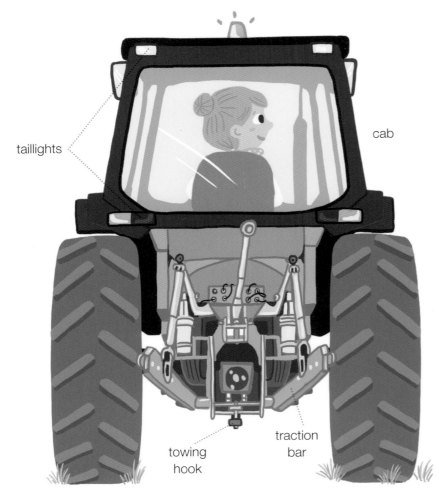

taillights

cab

towing hook

traction bar

Have you ever dreamed about operating a tractor, maybe one attached to a wagon, plow, or harrow?

The age requirement for driving a tractor on a farm depends on where you live. You may also need a special driver's license to drive on the road.

Children can ride in a tractor with a farmer at an educational farm. The farmer will show you how it works.

🧤 Tools

There are many tools that help prepare or tend the soil in a vegetable garden or field.

hoe

shovel

rake

spade

weeding hoe

string

watering can

bag of seeds

shears

brush cutter

basket

bulb planter

dibble

bucket

scythe

sickle

wheelbarrow

pitchfork

What
do you need to garden

Plants can be grown anywhere, whether in a backyard, a garden, a planter box, or even a flowerpot.

Farmers use special tools and equipment. But for plants grown in and around the home, there are smaller versions of these tools.

Hand trowels, hand forks, and pruning scissors are some of the tools that are a better fit for an indoor garden.

Permaculture Farm **70**
Educational Farm **72**

13

 Animals That Help

Some animals and little creatures can be very helpful to farmers.

Dogs guard the farm.

Cats chase rats.

Butterflies and bees pollinate fruit trees.

Owls hunt small animals.

Spiders feast on insects.

Ladybugs eat aphids.

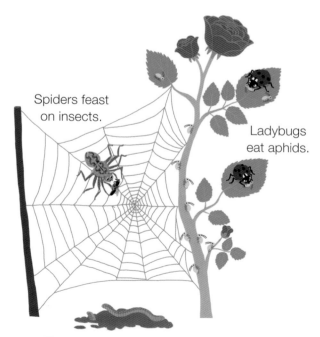

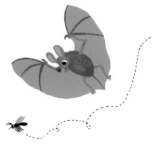

Bats feed on mosquitoes.

Earthworms help enrich the soil.

🐭 Pests

There are also animals and small critters that cause problems for farmers.

Foxes attack chickens.

Rodents nibble on grain.

Some beetles eat and damage crops.

Aphids weaken plants.

Slugs munch on vegetables.

What are pesticides?

Certain insects feed on the leaves or fruits of plants. To stop the insects, some farmers spray chemicals on the plants to kill the pests.

The chemicals, called pesticides, allow the plants to grow well, but they may be harmful to people.

Before they are eaten, fruits and vegetables need to be washed to get rid of the pesticides that might have been sprayed on them.

Maintaining the Field **48**
Permaculture Farm **70**

☁ Weather

Weather is an important factor in plant growth. Farmers pay close attention to what the weather will be to make sure the plants get the right amount of sun and water.

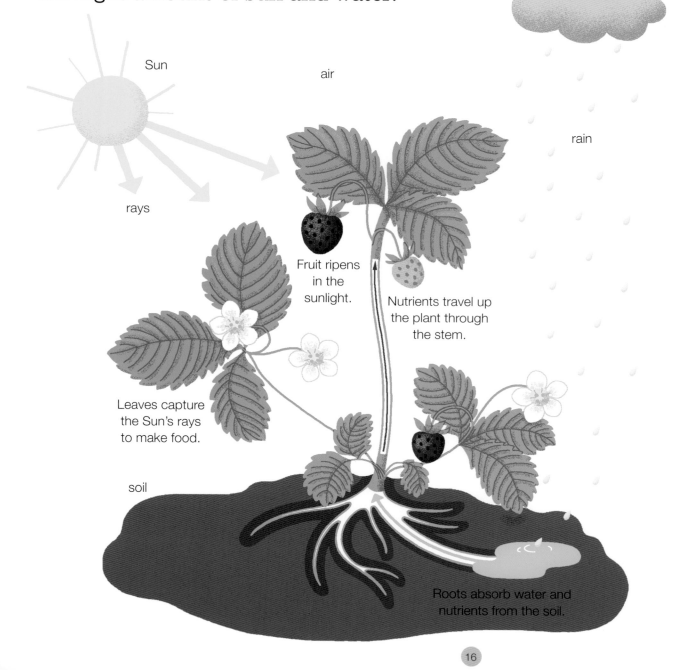

Sun

air

rain

rays

Fruit ripens in the sunlight.

Nutrients travel up the plant through the stem.

Leaves capture the Sun's rays to make food.

soil

Roots absorb water and nutrients from the soil.

In extreme weather conditions, farmers protect their crops in many ways.

drought

watering the fields

late frost

heating the orchard

hail

using anti-hail nets

wind

growing hedges

What
do plants need in order to grow

If you have plants at home, you know that you have to water them from time to time. Water is essential for a plant's growth and development.

But some plants, like cacti, need only a little bit of water. If they get too much, they die.

Plants also need sunlight to live. Don't leave your plants in a room that's too dark!

Maintaining the Field **48**
Fruits **56**

Let's Review!

Do you know the name of this vehicle? What is it used for?
Can you find the revolving light, running board, and exhaust pipe?

Do you remember what these tools are called? What do you think they are used for?

There are many animals on the farm.
Can you name some of them? If you have a pet
at home, would it be helpful on a farm?

Farm Animals

Poultry Yard

Many types of birds, including chickens, geese, and turkeys, are raised on farms.

goose eggs

feathers

straw

gander (male)

goose (female)

geese

gosling

grain

food trough

drake (male)

webbed feet

hen (female)

ducklings

ducks

pond

22

fox

fence

tom (male)

turkeys

wattle

hen (female)

helmet

drinking trough

rooster (male)

guinea fowl

chickens

chicks

worm

hen (female)

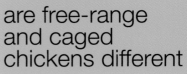

Some farms raise "free-range" chickens. These chickens are allowed to roam freely outdoors for part of the day.

Many chickens are raised in battery cages, which are cages that are stacked on top of one another. These cages are housed in large sheds.

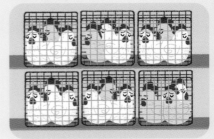

Caged chickens spend their whole lives confined to their small living spaces and are not allowed outdoors. This practice has been banned in some places.

🐔 Chicken Coop

Chickens are popular animals on the farm because they provide eggs, which are used to make all kinds of food.

hen preening, or smoothing its feathers

collecting eggs

comb

hard beak

wattles

large feathers

rooster

spur

four clawed toes

small wings

identification band

pecking at grain

sitting on egg to keep it warm

nest

Cochin

New Hampshire Red

Barred Rock

chick

Sussex

Why
is there no chick in my egg

?

Eggs can be tasty, whether they are scrambled, hard-boiled, or cooked as an omelet. You would not find a chick when you crack open an egg that you eat.

Hens reproduce and have babies when a rooster lives with them. The hens will keep the eggs warm until the chicks hatch.

The eggs we buy come from chickens that don't live with roosters. In this egg, there is only a clear liquid called egg white and a yellow yolk.

Poultry Yard **22**
Educational Farm **72**

Pigs

Also known as swine or hogs, pigs are some of the most intelligent animals in the world.

Landrace

ears that stand up

snout

Large White boar (male)

corkscrew tail

Duroc piglet

cloven, or two-toed hoof

teats

Large White sow (female)

Piétrain

Meishan

half-moon
shack

grains
and corn

mud puddle

food trough

water trough

heat lamp

sow nursing
her piglets

27

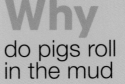

Why
do pigs roll
in the mud
?

Have you heard the phrase "eat like a pig" to describe a messy eater? The truth is that pigs are not messy at all!

They are actually some of the cleanest animals on the farm. When they roll in the mud, it's not to get dirty.

The pigs are really keeping cool and protecting their skin. The mud creates a layer that keeps bugs and heat away from their bodies.

Raising Cows

On a farm, cows graze on grass, but they also eat alfalfa, hay, and grains.

pasture

machine milking

hand milking

livestock barn

feeding

filling up with hay

tanker

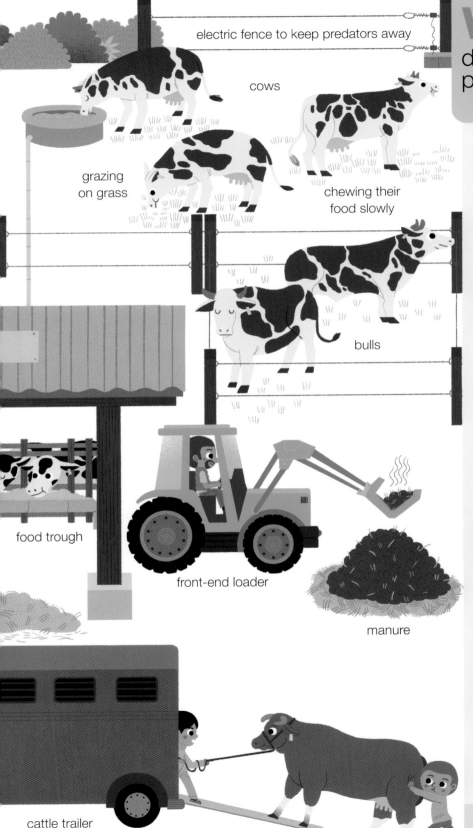

electric fence to keep predators away

cows

grazing
on grass

chewing their
food slowly

bulls

food trough

front-end loader

manure

cattle trailer

?

Like all female mammals, cows produce milk right after their calves are born. They give birth to one calf a year.

On some farms, cows are allowed to nurse their young, or provide calves with their own milk.

Cows are raised on farms for their milk or their meat.

🐂 Types of Cows

Dairy cows are kept on farms to produce milk, while other cows are kept to produce beef.

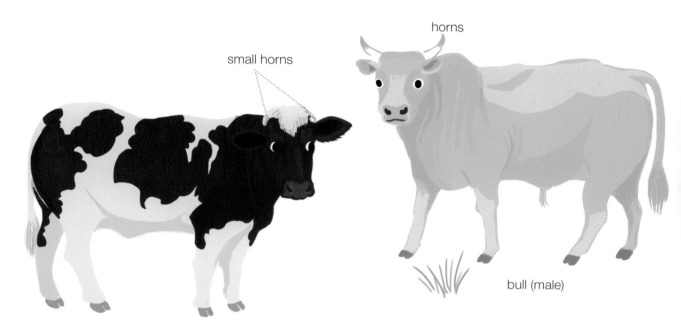

small horns

horns

bull (male)

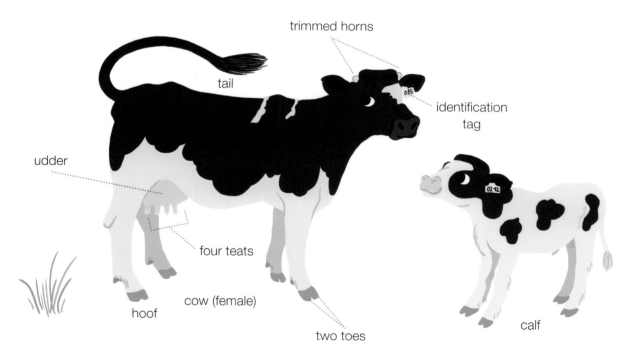

trimmed horns

tail

identification tag

udder

four teats

cow (female)

hoof

two toes

calf

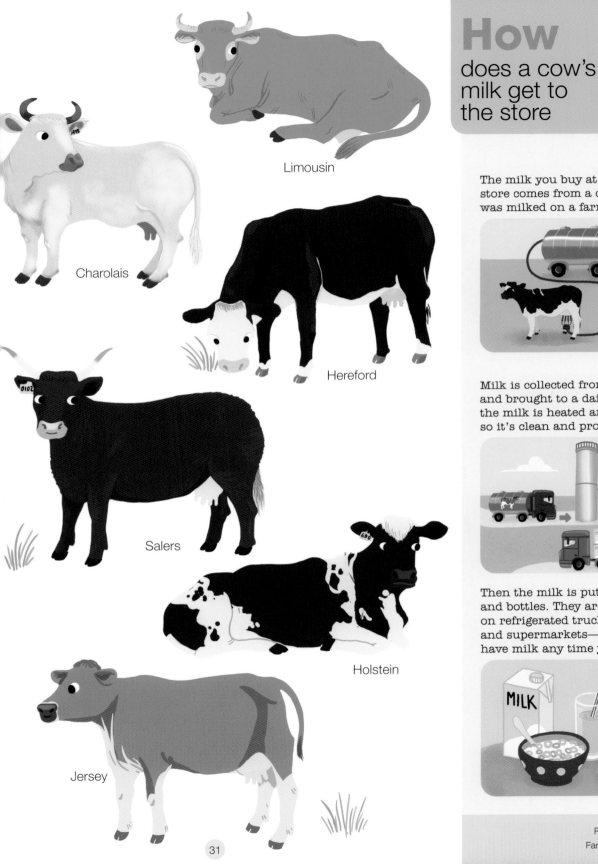

Limousin

Charolais

Hereford

Salers

Holstein

Jersey

How

does a cow's milk get to the store ?

The milk you buy at the grocery store comes from a cow that was milked on a farm.

Milk is collected from the farm and brought to a dairy. There, the milk is heated and filtered so it's clean and processed.

Then the milk is put in cartons and bottles. They are transported on refrigerated trucks to stores and supermarkets—so you can have milk any time you want!

MILK

Sheep and Goats

They are often kept together in a barn or pen, which is a small, fenced-in area.

hay

sheepdog

a flock of sheep

shearing a sheep

wool

a herd of goats

bottle-feeding
a lamb

hand milking

machine
milking

waiting
their turn

How
is wool made

?

When it's cold out, you might wear a wool sweater to keep warm. That wool comes from a sheep that was sheared.

Sheep are usually sheared once a year so they stay cool in the warmer months. After the wool is sheared, it is washed, rinsed, and spun into yarn.

The wool can be dyed with different colors and sold to sweater manufacturers. You could learn to knit too!

🐐 Types of Goats

Unlike cows and sheep, goats forage for food. They prefer woody plants, weeds, and hay.

thick hair

udder

beard

wattles

teats

cloven hoof

Provençal

female Alpine goat and kid

female Saanen goat and kid

climbing
a tree

Angora

Golden
Guernsey

How
is cheese made

?

Do you like cheese? Have you noticed that some are soft and easy to spread, while others are hard and need to be cut with a knife?

Cheese can be made from the milk of goats, cows, or sheep. An enzyme called rennet is often added to turn the milk into a more solid form called curds.

Salt is added to the cheese, which then sits in a mold to take shape. The cheese can be left to age for days, or even years!

Sheep and Goats **32**
Farmers Market **60**

Types of Sheep

Sheep are raised on farms for
their wool, milk, and meat.

lamb

ewe

wool

spiral horns

trimmed
tail

toothless
upper jaw

ram

cloven hoof

Lacaune

Suffolk

thick wool

Merino

Have you ever been given a special hat to wear on a field trip? It may not have been just to protect your eyes from the sun.

The hat was likely used to make it easier for teachers to keep track of you and every child on the trip. It's the same reason why farmers color their sheep.

Using marking fluid or paint, farmers can quickly tell which sheep is theirs and bring them safely home.

✖ Health Care

Farmers take daily care of their animals, but veterinarians are called when these creatures get sick or injured.

veterinary truck

vet box for medical supplies

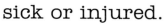

veterinarian taking an ultrasound image

veterinary team operating on a cow

attaching a tag

vaccinating

listening

helping a ewe give birth

How
do you become a veterinarian

?

If you have an interest in animals and taking care of their health, you might consider becoming a veterinarian.

You would need to attend veterinary school to learn about animals, what their needs are, and how best to take care of them.

You may travel from one farm to another to help farmers take care of their livestock.

The Farm 8

Let's Review!

Sheep are usually sheared once a year. Do you know why?
Can you put these three steps in order?

Can you name these birds that live in the poultry yard? Look at the dotted lines on a few of them.
What are these special features called?

Can you tell the difference between a pig, a cow, and a goat? How?

Veterinarians are doctors who take care of animals.
Would you like to be one?
Which animal would you like to learn more about?

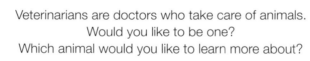

Crops

Preparing the Soil

Before crops are planted in a field, farmers have to prepare the soil to ensure that the plants will grow well.

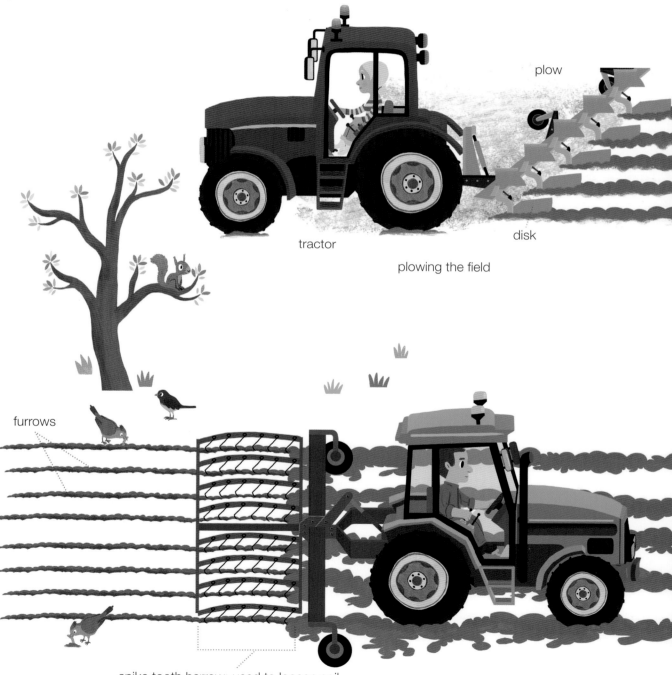

plow

disk

tractor

plowing the field

furrows

spike tooth harrow: used to loosen soil

44

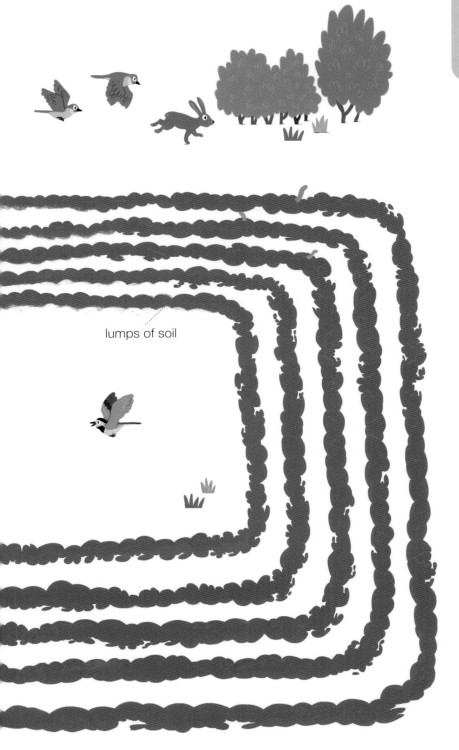

lumps of soil

Soil can be hard, and seeds planted in unplowed soil might not be able to take root. They would also be left exposed for birds to eat.

By plowing the field, the farmer breaks the hard crust of the ground and allows nutrients, oxygen, and moisture to pass easily through the soil.

Settled into the soil, the seeds find all they need to grow into healthy plants—especially with adequate water and sunlight!

Tractor **10**
Tools **12**

🌱 Sowing

After the field is plowed, the farmer enriches the soil with fertilizer before putting seeds into the soil.

plowed soil

tractor

planter

dropping seeds into the soil

fertilizer: a mixture of straw and animal poop

manure spreader

furrows

Where

do seeds come from ?

Seeds can be found inside many fruits and vegetables. If these seeds are planted, they'll grow and produce more fruits and vegetables.

While saving seeds from one crop to use in the next growing season is a good idea, most farmers find it more convenient to buy seeds from farm suppliers.

SEEDS

Seed companies produce all sorts of seeds. Some specialize in heirloom seeds, from plants that have been grown for a long time. Others create new varieties.

Tractor 10

Preparing the Soil 44

🪣 Maintaining the Field

For crops to grow well, they need to be watered and monitored regularly.

spraying pesticide

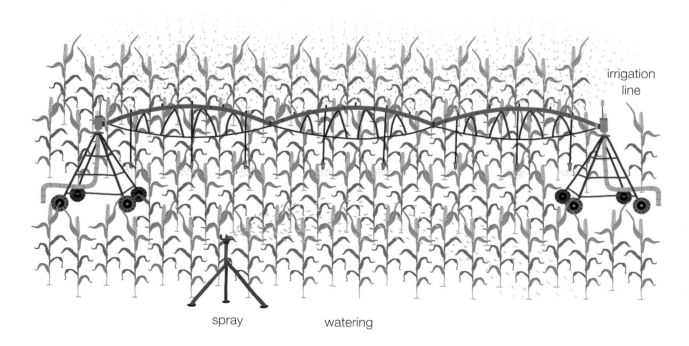

irrigation line

spray   watering

inspecting the crops

monitoring amount of
moisture in the soil

repairing the fence

What
does "organic" mean ?

You might have heard of vegetables or products, like bread and cereal, being "organic." They can be found at farmers markets and supermarkets.

Organic vegetables and fruits are generally grown using very little or no pesticides or chemicals.

Organic meat comes from animals fed with organically grown foods or housed in natural living conditions.

Weather **16**
Permaculture Farm **70**

Harvesting

When the wheat crops are ripe, they are quickly harvested while the weather is good. Some crops are even harvested at night.

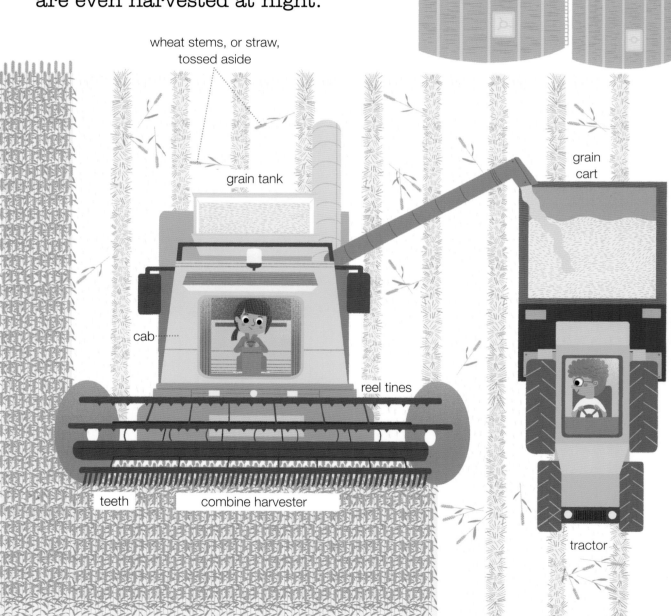

silos for storing grain

wheat stems, or straw, tossed aside

grain tank

grain cart

cab

reel tines

teeth

combine harvester

tractor

straw barn

straw baler

bale of straw

When you travel through the countryside at the end of the summer, you see huge cylinders or cubes of straw sitting in the fields.

That straw will serve as bedding for livestock. When the straw gets dirty, the farmer changes it.

The animals can eat straw, but they prefer hay, which is tall, dried grass that is more tender than straw.

Cereals

Cereal crops are also called grain crops. They are an important food source for people all over the world.

rice

common
wheat

durum
wheat

barley

What
can be made with cereals

You may eat cereal for breakfast. The cereal flakes in your bowl are made from grains that grew in a field, then were processed and packaged at a factory.

Ground into flour, cereal grains can be made into bread, cakes, pasta, and many other foods.

Cereal grains are also used to feed many of the animals that are raised on a farm.

oat

rye

corn

Harvesting **50**

Rice Farm **68**

Vegetables

Vegetable farms grow many types of vegetables.

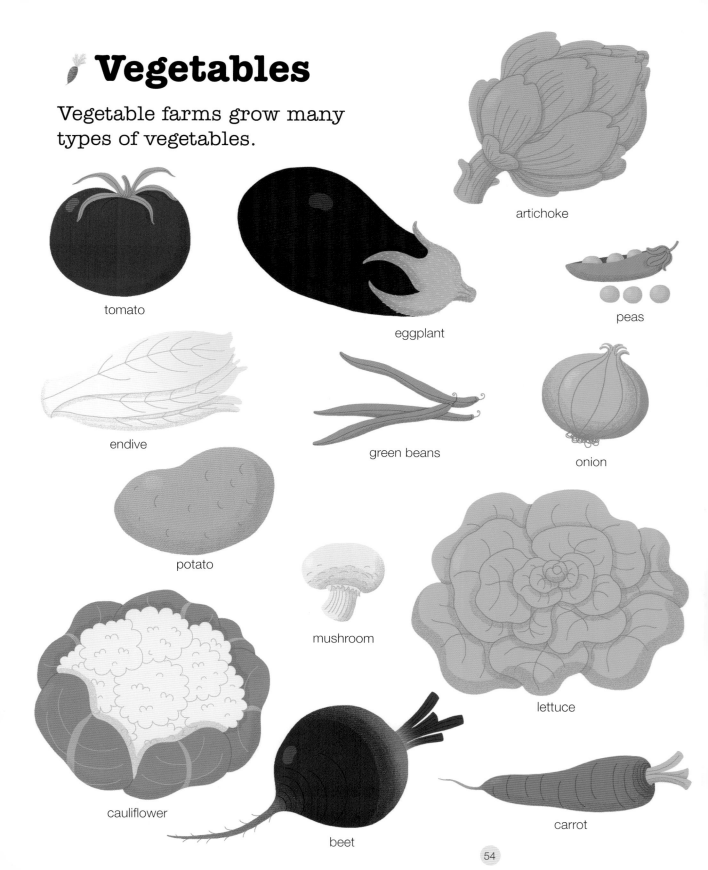

artichoke

tomato

eggplant

peas

endive

green beans

onion

potato

mushroom

lettuce

cauliflower

beet

carrot

supported by garden stakes

underground

like a flower

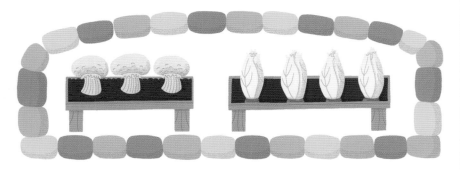

in the dark

Why
are vegetables covered

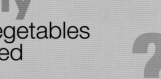

You may have seen fields with long rows of vegetables covered by plastic sheets.

Farmers use these covers to protect the vegetables from rain and snow, weeds, and small animals like slugs.

The covers also help trap the heat of the sun and keep the soil moist. This way, the vegetables will certainly grow well and be healthy!

Greenhouse **58**
Farmers Market **60**

Fruits

In an orchard, fruits grow on trees, bushes, and vines.

strawberry

strawberry bushes

raspberry

raspberry bush

rhubarb

rhubarb plant

blueberry

blueberry bush

cantaloupe

cantaloupe vine

watermelon

watermelon vine

pear

pear tree

kiwi

kiwi vine

apple   apple tree

plum   plum tree

cherry   cherry tree

apricot   apricot tree

peach   peach tree

fig   fig tree

banana   banana tree

orange   orange tree

Where
are fruits grown ?

Different types of fruit are grown all over the world: The mangoes you eat may come from India, kiwis from New Zealand, and pineapples from Brazil.

Fruits are often transported by ship. They are packed in protective containers that keep them from spoiling during long journeys.

That is why at the market you may see locally grown fruit being sold next to fruit that comes from places far away.

Greenhouse 58
Farmers Market 60

Greenhouse

In this controlled environment, farmers can grow plants year-round without worrying about extreme weather or temperature conditions.

The glass walls and roof conserve heat and provide protection from rain and snow.

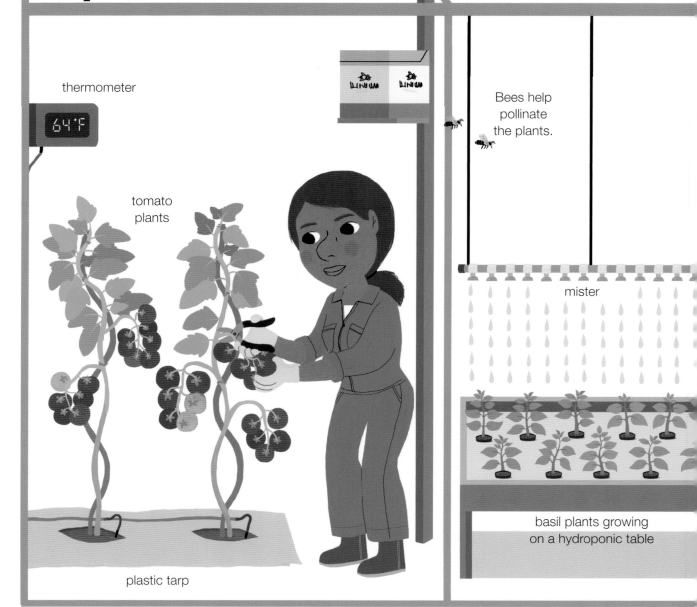

thermometer

64°F

Bees help pollinate the plants.

tomato plants

mister

basil plants growing on a hydroponic table

plastic tarp

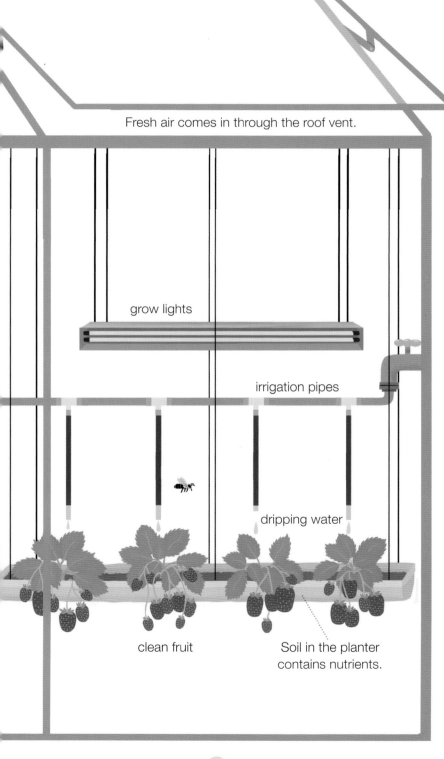

Fresh air comes in through the roof vent.

grow lights

irrigation pipes

dripping water

clean fruit

Soil in the planter contains nutrients.

When
are fruits ready to be picked

?

Plants are sensitive to light, temperature, and the amount of moisture in the soil. They know when to bloom and grow, and when to conserve energy.

Fruits—as well as vegetables, flowers, and trees—grow according to the season, and at different times of the year.

In tropical climates, there are wet and dry seasons. Some plants, such as coconuts and papayas, bear fruit year-round. Others, such as lychees, are seasonal.

Farmers Market

Many cities and towns host a farmers market once or twice a week. Farmers go there to sell their products.

awning

free-range chicken

zucchini

bell peppers

potatoes

eggs

yogurt

tomatoes

shallots

carr

cheeses

canopy

cantaloupe

vegetables in jars

organic products

BIO

BIO

jams

honey

nectarines

crates of potatoes

scale

0.00   0.00

cucumber

lettuce

parsley

pear

celery

apples

asparagus

leek

plums

bread

cereal

How
are farmers markets different from supermarkets ?

Fruits and vegetables, cheese, meat, and eggs . . . You'll find many of these products at the farmers market, as well as at the supermarket.

Products at farmers markets come directly from local farmers. They have been handled less and have traveled a shorter distance to get to you.

Products at supermarkets usually travel a long way to get to customers. The prices can include the costs of processing, packaging, and transportation.

Vegetables **54**
Fruits **56**

Let's Review!

Do you know what the farmer is doing in each of these images?

Do you know the names of these vegetables and how they grow?
Which ones grow underground? Do any of them grow in the dark?

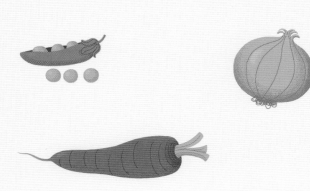

What are the names of these fruits? Is one of them your favorite?
Would you pick them from a vine, a tree, or a bush?

Have you been to a farmers market? What did you buy?
What would you sell if you were a farmer?

Special Farms

🐝 Apiary

An apiary, or bee yard, is where beekeepers raise bees and collect their honey.

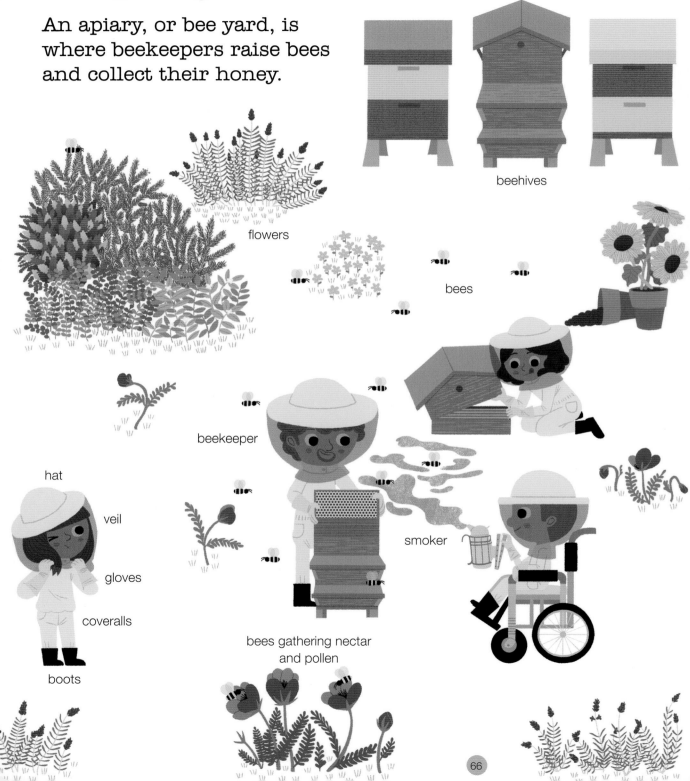

beehives

flowers

bees

beekeeper

bees gathering nectar and pollen

hat

veil

gloves

coveralls

boots

smoker

honey house

honeycomb

frame

centrifuge

honey drum

shop

beeswax candles

jars of honey

honey candy

honey pastry

gingerbread

royal jelly

honey drink

pollen

POLLEN
POLLEN POLLEN

soaps

Around the world, bees perform an important task: pollinating flowers and grains so fruits, nuts, and cereals can grow.

However, there are fewer bees than before for a number of reasons, including changes in climate, pollution, use of pesticides, and loss of habitat.

As more rural land is transformed to urban areas, bees have to compete with other insects to gather nectar and pollen.

Animals That Help **14**
Permaculture Farm **70**

Rice Farm

Rice is a cereal grain that's grown in partly flooded fields called paddies.

rice seeds

sowing

flooding the field

transplanting seedlings

flowering

harvesting

🌼 Nurseries

Before being sold at a flower shop or garden center, flowering plants are grown at specialized farms.

tree nursery

fir trees

tree ready to be sold

tulip field

cut flowers

harvesting lavender

greenhouse

repotting

putting in stakes

pansies

cacti

Flowers are commonly used to beautify homes and gardens. Their colors and scents create a welcoming and cheerful atmosphere.

FLORIST

Flowers are also used to make medicines and perfumes. The scents or oils can be extracted by heating or through the addition of chemicals.

Did you know that some flowers can be eaten as well? Nasturtiums in a salad make a nutritious meal: They're full of vitamin C!

Permaculture Farm

Permaculture farmers grow food and raise animals in an environmentally friendly way, without using chemicals or machinery.

relying on animal power

mule

free-range livestock

vole

kingfisher

moorhen

pond

tree stump

Many types of animals share the space.

pile of rocks

toad

ground beetle

grass snake

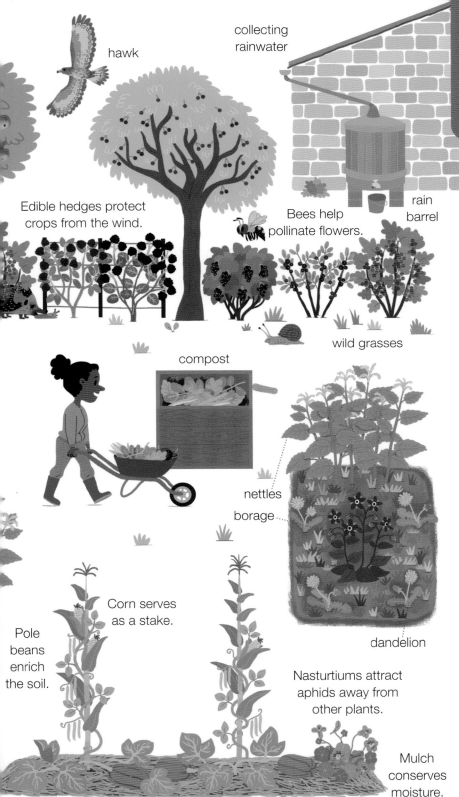

hawk

collecting rainwater

Edible hedges protect crops from the wind.

Bees help pollinate flowers.

rain barrel

wild grasses

compost

nettles

borage

dandelion

Corn serves as a stake.

Pole beans enrich the soil.

Nasturtiums attract aphids away from other plants.

Mulch conserves moisture.

Squash leaves provide shade.

companion plants

How

is permaculture farming different ?

When you visit farming areas, you may see vast fields of one type of crop. This has been the most common way to grow large quantities of crops.

However, permaculture and sustainable farming can also produce large quantities of food by creating a diverse natural environment.

Different types of plants are grown together to help one another. This is seen as being beneficial to people, plants, and animals.

Animals That Help **14**

Weather **16**

Educational Farm

Visitors can learn all about farm animals, work, and life.

orchard

tour guide

compost bin

beehives

scarecrow

vegetable garden

sitting on a tractor

feeding chickens

horse

collecting eggs

geese

ducks

pond

donkey

picking apples

grinding apples into pulp

pressing out juice with an apple press

activity leader

tasting the apple juice

milking a goat

cows

You may be able to go on a field trip to an educational farm with your school. These farms are open to the public.

EDUCATIONAL FARM

The farmers talk about the many tasks they have, and what they need to do to grow and raise fruits, vegetables, and animals.

Visiting a farm helps us better understand where our food comes from and how important farmwork is.

The Farm 8
Apiary 66

Let's Review!

Can you name the items the beekeeper has to wear while working in the apiary?
Where do the bees go after collecting nectar and pollen?

There are many steps to growing rice. Can you put these steps in order?

On what type of farm would you see these activities and objects?

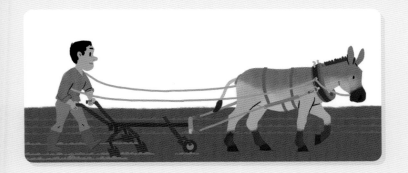

Have you ever been to a farm?
Have you tried helping the farmers out?
Which job would you like to do?

Index

DO YOU KNOW?™ series

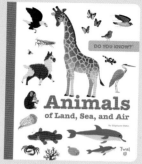

978-2-40803-356-9

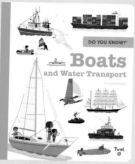

978-2-40804-255-4

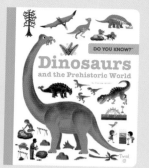

978-2-40802-467-3

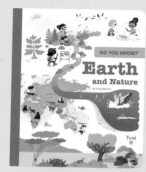

978-2-40803-357-6

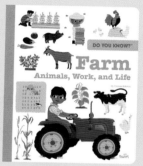

978-2-40804-988-1

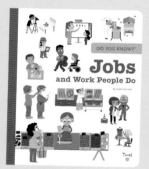

978-2-40803-753-6

978-2-40804-253-0

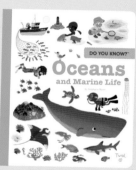

978-2-40802-466-6

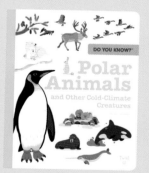

978-2-40804-620-0

978-2-40802-916-6

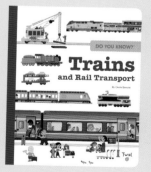

978-2-40803-755-0

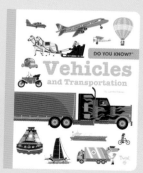

978-2-40802-915-9